A QUAKER CUPBOARD

BEING A FRIENDLY COLLECTION OF

BIBLE VERSES, QUERIES

AND FRIENDLY VOICES IN PROSE AND POEMS

ON

THE QUAKER TESTIMONIES OF SPICES

SIMPLICITY

PEACE

INTEGRITY

COMMUNITY

EQUALITY

STEWARDSHIP

BY
DAVID MADDEN

"Dearly beloved Friends, these things we do not lay upon you as a rule or form to walk by, but that all, with the measure of light which is pure and holy may be guided; and so in the Light walking and abiding, these things may be fulfilled in the Spirit, not from the letter, for the letter killeth, but the Spirit giveth life."

Letter from the Meeting of Quaker Elders at Balby in Yorkshire, England: 1656

TABLE OF CONTENTS

Meetinghouse of the Westerly (RI) Monthly Meeting of the
Religious Society of Friends

INTRODUCTION

The concept of "The Inner Light" is the foundation of Quaker faith and practice. This metaphor is known by other names such as "The Light of God", "The Light Within", and "The Inward Light." Regardless of what it is called, the idea remains the same: God's dwelling place is within each of us. While scripture and testimonies from others can be and often are helpful as a guide on our faith journeys, such writings are ultimately not necessary. God speaks today and will in years to come as surely as God did to those living in the times of the Bible and in the centuries since then.

This was the idea that Margaret Fell heard when her future husband, George Fox, delivered his sermon at the Ulverston steeple-house in 1694. She recorded the first time she heard him speak as follows:

> "And so he went on, and said, 'That Christ was the Light of the world, and lighteth every man that cometh into the world; and that by this light they might be gathered to God,' &c. I stood up in my pew, and wondered at his doctrine, for I had never heard such before. And then he went on, and opened the scriptures, and said, 'The scriptures were the prophets' words, and Christ's and the apostles' words, and what, as they spoke, they enjoyed and possessed, and had it from the Lord': and said, 'Then what had any to do with the scriptures, but as they came to the Spirit that gave them forth? You will say, Christ saith this, and the apostles say this; but what canst thou say? Art thou a child of the Light, and hast thou walked in the Light, and what thou speakest, is it inwardly from God?' &c. This opened me so, that it cut me to the heart; and then I saw clearly we were all wrong. So I sat down in my pew again, and cried bitterly: and I cried in my spirit to the Lord, 'We are all thieves; we are all thieves; we have taken the scriptures in words, and know nothing of them in ourselves.'"
> *From "The testimony of Margaret Fox concerning her late husband, "The Journal of George Fox, 1694*

"What canst thou say?" This is the question at the heart of Quakerism. It is not enough for us to rely solely on others; we are to seek after God in our own experiences, thoughts and feelings. To do otherwise is to be a "thief" who takes another's experience of God as his or her own.

When a person believes the presence of the divine is available within him/herself, the need for clergy, creed, scripture or sanctuary is greatly diminished. Such a highly individualistic approach could have meant that Quakerism would not last very long after the deaths of its founders, George Fox and Margaret Fell. However, unlike the Ranters, a similar religious group that believed God is found in every creature and that also formed in England around the same time, Quakerism has survived for over 350 years.

This is due in large part to the fact that, as much as Quakers value the mystical experience of directly finding "the inner light of God" in each individual's heart, we also place a high degree of emphasis on the importance of community centered in the local Monthly Meeting, as we call our congregations.

> "Mysticism exists in all religions; every great world religion has its mystical sect or groups. What the Quakers, as mystics, are to Christianity, the Zen (or Chan) sect is to Buddhism, the Yogis are to Hinduism, the Sufis to Mohammedanism, and the Taoists to the religion of China. But Oriental mysticism, like Oriental religion in general, is individualistic…Quakerism is peculiar in being a group mysticism, grounded in Christian concepts."
> *Howard H. Brinton, Friends for 350 Years, Pendle Hill Publications, 2002, pp. xix-xx*

A sense of community that emphasizes the paramount importance of the individual as the bearer of the "Inner Light" but that also affirms the importance of a corporate identity is made possible by what Quakers refer to as the testimonies. Testimonies are the record of the ways Quakers have attempted to put our faith into practice in the living of our daily lives according to values, convictions and principles that are seen to be in accord with the "Inner Light". Unlike the way in which scripture is often viewed, the testimonies are not meant to be seen as being true at all times and for all circumstances. Neither are they to be seen as directly emanating from a supranatural entity. Rather, the testimonies spring from the experiences of human beings who are striving, often with difficulty and sometimes with failure, to face the dilemmas of life with courage and resolve. The testimonies are to be received, not as divine revelations, but as examples of how others before us have faced challenges and as a source of encouragement for facing our own with similar conviction.

The origins of Quakerism are deeply rooted in the tenets of Christianity. However, in a faith tradition that has historically placed so much emphasis on the individual, it is only to be expected that there would be a wide range of spiritual expression among Quakers today. So while there are Friends who hold to a Christocentric perspective, there are also Quakers who consider themselves to be Universalist in nature. As well as birthright Friends and those who have come originally from various Christian denominations, a Meeting might include people whose religious upbringing leads them to self-identify as Jewish Quakers, Wiccan Quakers, Taoist Quakers or Buddhist Quakers.

Diversity is found in corporate worship as well. Some Friends' worship services are much like a traditional Protestant service, in that there is a pastor who leads worship with hymns, prayers, and sermon, all with a strong emphasis on the authority of scripture as found in the Judeo-Christian Bible. Many other meetings worship in the unprogrammed tradition. This is a time of gathering together in silent waiting, with an expectation of hearing the "still, small voice of God". It is possible for the entire hour to pass in deeply spiritual silent worship or it may happen that a Friend will feel called to share a message arising out of the prompting of the Spirit. After discerning if the message is a genuine ministry, he or she will stand, speak plainly and briefly, and then sit down to return, with the rest of the meeting, to silence. After time for reflection, another message may be inspired by the previous words or another message entirely may follow, or the deep spiritual silence may continue unbroken until the hour closes with the person appointed to have care for the meeting shaking the hand of a person close by. In all this, an unprogrammed meeting takes to heart the Psalmist's words:

"Be still, and know that I am God" (Psalm 46:10 NIV)

For both individuals and institutions, life is a process of constant change and, because the testimonies are rooted in daily life, it is only to be expected that they should change as well. The core of the testimonies exists today, as it always has, in the command:

> "Love the Lord your God with all your passion and prayer and muscle and intelligence—and that you love your neighbor as well as you do yourself."
> *Luke 10:27 (The Message)*

However, particular aspects of the testimonies have changed as the times have changed. Quakers nowadays, for the most part, dress in a manner that makes them indistinguishable from others in society. We go to plays, movies and ballgames, listen to popular music, and rarely if ever address each other as "thee".

Howard Brinton, the prominent 20th century Quaker thinker, provided the Religious Society of Friends with a sense of continuity when he "rediscovered" the Quaker Testimonies of Simplicity, Peace, Integrity, Community, Equality, and Stewardship (sometimes Service), often referred to by the acronym SPICES. For many Quakers, these testimonies offer three important functions:

1. A reference for explaining basic Friendly beliefs to someone who associates Quakers mostly with cereal products and motor oil
2. A means for binding ourselves together in a fellowship that seeks to recognize and rely on God's presence in the ongoing process of daily life
3. A discipline for living fully in the present day while being mindful of the past influences on our identity

Each of the SPICES sections in A Quaker Cupboard contains Bible verses pertaining to that testimony along with queries from some of the Yearly Meetings found throughout the United States. Queries are questions that have long been used to guide Friends in examining the best way for meetings and individuals to live lives of simplicity, peace, integrity; to see all people as having the light of God within them and to serve others as we feel called. Each section also contains the voices of "weighty" Friends speaking in prose and poems on the truths that have comprised Quaker thought for over 350 years.

Westerly RI July 2011

SIMPLICITY

TESTIMONY ON SIMPLICITY

There is certainty among Friends that the world offers many distractions from the Truth, for example the pursuit of wealth or power or pleasure, extravagance in language, fashion or behavior, and too great an emphasis on business, even for good causes. Truth is usually discovered in quiet, undistracted waiting for its leadings in the human heart, in the humble simplicity of spirit which acknowledges that ultimately God is in charge of our world, not we ourselves.

The testimony of simplicity seeks, therefore, to focus our attention on what is essential and eternal, without distraction by the transitory or the trivial. Plain and honest speech is an expression of simplicity. Respect for God's creation and, therefore, concern for the environment and the right use of the world's resources is another obvious expression of this testimony. A growth economy based on extravagance, wastefulness and artificially stimulated wants is seen to be a fundamental violation of the testimony of simplicity.

Swarthmore Friends Meeting

SCRIPTURE ON SIMPLICITY

A pretentious, showy life is an empty life;
a plain and simple life is a full life. *Proverbs 13:7*

But he's already made it plain how to live, what to do,
what God is looking for in men and women.
It's quite simple: Do what is fair and just to your neighbor,
Be compassionate and loyal in your love,
And don't take yourself too seriously—
take God seriously. *Micah 6:8*

And when you come before God, don't turn that into a theatrical production either.
All these people making a regular show out of their prayers, hoping for stardom! Do
you think God sits in a box seat? Here's what I want you to do: Find a quiet, secluded
place so you won't be tempted to role-play before God. Just be there as simply and
honestly as you can manage. The focus will shift from you to God, and you will begin
to sense his grace. *Matthew 6:5-6*

Jesus called over a child, whom he stood in the middle of the room, and said, "I'm
telling you, once and for all, that unless you return to square one and start over like
children, you're not even going to get a look at the kingdom, let alone get in. Whoever
becomes simple and elemental again, like this child, will rank high in God's kingdom.
What's more, when you receive the childlike on my account, it's the same as receiving
me." *Matthew 18:2-3*

A devout life does bring wealth, but it's the rich simplicity of being yourself before
God. Since we entered the world penniless and will leave it penniless, if we have bread
on the table and shoes on our feet, that's enough. *1 Timothy 6:6-8*

Above all, my brothers and sisters, do not swear—not by heaven or by earth or by
anything else. All you need to say is a simple "Yes" or "No." Otherwise you will be
condemned. *James 5:12*

3

YEARLY MEETING QUERIES ON SIMPLICITY

What in my present life most distracts me from God? *Baltimore Yearly Meeting*

How do I discern what constitutes simplicity for me? *Earlham College*

How do I show my commitment to simplicity as an individual and as a part of a community? *Earlham College*

Do you take care that your spiritual growth is not sacrificed to busyness but instead integrates your life's activities? *New England Yearly Meeting*

Are you free from the burden of unnecessary possessions? *Northwest Yearly Meeting*

Do I choose with care the use of technology and devices that truly simplify and add quality to my life without adding an undue burden to essential resources? *Philadelphia Yearly Meeting*

Do we keep to simplicity and moderation in speech manner of living and vocation? *Southeastern Yearly Meeting*

FRIENDLY VOICES ON SIMPLICITY

Let the guest sojourning here know that in this home our life is simple. What we cannot afford we do not offer, but what good cheer we can give...we give gladly.
In a Quaker home, author unknown

Simplicity is not just simple clothes and a simple lifestyle. It's an organization of the mind that enables you to sort out the unimportant details that often clutter your thoughts.
Sidwell Friends 7th grader from Sidwell Friends Testimonials 2002

Personal pride does not end with noble blood. It leads people to a fond value of their persons, especially if they have any pretence to shape or beauty. Some are so taken with themselves it would seem that nothing else deserved their attention. Their folly would diminish if they could spare but half the time to think of God, that they spend in washing, perfuming, painting and dressing their bodies. In these things they are precise and very artificial and spare no cost. But what aggravates the evil is that the pride of one might comfortably supply the needs of ten. Gross impiety it is that a nation's pride should be maintained in the face of its poor.
William Penn No Cross No Crown

I saw that a humble man, with the Blessing of the Lord, might live on a little, and that where the heart was set on greatness, success in business did not satisfy the craving; but that commonly with an increase of wealth, the desire for wealth increased. There was a care on my mind so to pass my time, as to things outward, that nothing might hinder me from the most steady attention to the voice of the True Shepherd.
John Woolman c. 1744

The doctrine of simplicity, in so far as it meant absence of superfluity, was the source of most of the Quaker educational innovations. In the days when the curriculum was largely based upon the classics, mathematics and other subjects designed primarily to polish and adorn, the Quaker schools emphasized practical subjects.

George Fox set up the first Quaker schools in 1668 to teach "whatsoever things are civil and useful in creation." Quaker schools were among the earliest, if not actually the first, to introduce science into the curriculum. In the days when trades were learned by apprenticeship to a master craftsman, the Quaker schools gave instruction in applied sciences. It was natural that a religious body which believed in a religion based in experience should relate education to that which can be experienced.
Howard H. Brinton, Friends for 350 Years, Pendle Hill Publications, 2002, p. 183

Voluntary simplicity involves both inner and outer condition. It means singleness of purpose, sincerity and honesty within, as well as avoidance of exterior clutter, of many possessions irrelevant to the chief purpose of life. It means an ordering and guiding of our energy and our desires, a partial restraint in some directions in order to secure greater abundance of life in other directions. It involves a deliberate organization of life for a purpose.
Richard B Gregg "The Value of Voluntary Simplicity" Pendle Hill Pamphlet #3 P4

There is no fixed standard of simplicity. What is very simple for one person often seems very complex and extravagant for another person. There is no known calculus of simplicity. Simplicity at its best and truest is this utter honesty of heart and life, this complete sincerity of soul before God and in relation with our fellowmen so that we truly struggle to be what we tell God we want to be and what we profess in our social relations to be.
Rufus Jones "Rethinking Quaker Principles" Pendle Hill Pamphlet # 8 P15

To attain to simplicity is first of all to have a single sublime purpose in life, and second it is to order all one's time, thought, and possessions so that they may contribute to, rather than hinder, our progress toward that sublime goal.
Gilbert Kilpack "Our Hearts Are Restless" Pendle Hill Pamphlet #32 P14

The absence of ritualistic symbols in Quaker worship is in accord with simplicity because, either that which is symbolized is present, in which case the symbol may be considered superfluous, or if that which is symbolized is not present, the symbol may become a misleading substitute.
Howard H. Brinton "The Nature of Quakerism" Pendle Hill Pamphlet #49 P8&9

Sonnet for Coming Home
16 February 1992

Let me sing praises to familiar things
That punctuate the dailyness of life,
Free from excitement, novelty, and strife;
Bed, breakfast, dinner, lunch, old wedding rings,
The daily paper that the morning brings,
The cup and saucer, spoon and fork and knife,
And most of all, my long-beloved wife.
Outside, a squirrel jumps, a small bird sings.

I have indeed adventured round this earth
Of which I consider myself a citizen;
I love its vast variety, but when
I travel home again, the precious worth,
The endless wonder of the commonplace
Fills up my smiling soul with joy and grace.

Kenneth Boulding

If you keep the green bough in your heart
The singing bird will come
China

PEACE

TESTIMONY ON PEACE

The peace testimony is based on the same understanding of the nature of God and of human beings. How can one kill another child of God, a potential channel of Truth, no matter how misguided he or she may seem at the moment? This testimony has led Friends to oppose all wars and preparation for wars. At the time of the American Revolution, many Friends were 'disowned' by their Meetings for participating in military actions. Later, Friends, faced with military conscription, worked to establish the right of conscientious objection. Some Friends today work to end the conscription for military purposes not only of their bodies but also of their tax money.

The peace testimony has meant efforts to ease suffering of victims of war on all sides. It means efforts to be or to seek a reconciling force between peoples and nations in conflict. It means a constant search for nonviolent means of conflict resolution through institutions of law, such as international treaties and structures like the European Union or the United Nations. It means a continuing search for peace and social justice through personal and group nonviolent techniques for mediation and social change. The Friends Committee on National Legislation (FCNL) in Washington, D.C., and the Quaker United Nations Offices (QUNOs) in Geneva and New York, for example, promote Quaker views at the heart of centers of power, where political, economic and military decisions with worldwide effect are made ("speaking truth to power").
Swarthmore Friends Meeting

SCRIPTURE ON PEACE

A meal of bread and water in contented peace is better than a banquet spiced with quarrels. *Proverbs 17:1*

One handful of peaceful repose
Is better than two fistfuls of worried work. *Ecclesiastes 4:6*

You're familiar with the old written law, 'Love your friend,' and its unwritten companion, 'Hate your enemy.' I'm challenging that. I'm telling you to love your enemies. Let them bring out the best in you, not the worst. When someone gives you a hard time, respond with the energies of prayer, for then you are working out of your true selves, your God-created selves. *Matthew 5:43-45*

Don't fret or worry. Instead of worrying, pray. Let petitions and praises shape your worries into prayers, letting God know your concerns. Before you know it, a sense of God's wholeness, everything coming together for good, will come and settle you down. It's wonderful what happens when Christ displaces worry at the center of your life. *Philippians 4:6-7*

Be agreeable, be sympathetic, be loving, be compassionate, be humble. That goes for all of you, no exceptions. No retaliation. No sharp-tongued sarcasm. Instead, bless— that's your job, to bless. You'll be a blessing and also get a blessing. *1 Peter 3:8-9*

YEARLY MEETING QUERIES ON PEACE

As we work for peace in the world, are we nourished by peace within and among ourselves? *Baltimore Yearly Meeting*

Do I think about power: who has it, and how it should be used? Am I careful to use my own power for just and constructive ends? *Earlham College*

When discouraged, do you remember that Jesus said, "Peace is my parting gift to you, my own peace, such the world cannot give. Set your troubled hearts at rest, and banish your fears"? John 14:27 *New England Yearly Meeting*

Are we exerting our influence in favor of settlement of all differences by truly nonviolent methods? *New York Yearly Meeting*

Do you observe and teach the Friends testimony against military training and service, making clear that war is incompatible with the spirit and teachings of the Gospel? *Northwest Yearly Meeting*

Do I treat conflict as an opportunity for growth, and address it with careful attention? *Philadelphia Yearly Meeting*

Do we seek consistently to carry out this testimony for peace in all our relationships, including family, community, and work life? *Southeastern Yearly Meeting*

FRIENDLY VOICES ON PEACE

There is no way to peace - peace is the way. *A.J. Muste*

The first step to peace is to stand still in the Light. *George Fox: To all that would know the way to the kingdom, pamphlet, 1653*

May we look upon our treasures, and the furniture of our houses, and [our] garments, and try whether the seeds of war have any nourishment in these our possessions. *John Woolman*

The national holidays of all countries celebrate military occasions; the national heroes are the leaders of war. Nelson, Wellington, Napoleon, Washington and Lincoln, may differ in personal virtue but they have in common one thing that makes them heroes: their leadership in war. The national ritual centers around the military parade, the salute to the flag, the remembrance of war dead. Even religion, where it subordinates itself to national emotion, becomes entangled more and more in military trappings. The cross on the altar is obscured by regimental flags, the gospel of universal love is drowned in the prayer for victory, and the humble ministers of Christ go forth in gorgeous array to bless the instruments of death.
Kenneth Boulding "New Nations for Old" Pendle Hill Pamphlet #17 p17

We want peace- but our financial security, our gracious, quiet homes are this moment dependent upon the industries of war. We know that the roots of war reach into every suburb and every home and that those roots would wither and die if we did not feed them with a publicly accepted everyday brand of human selfishness.
Gilbert Kilpack "Our Hearts Are Restless" Pendle Hill Pamphlet #32 P11

13

Harmony is in some respects a better word than "pacifism" which has acquired an unfortunate negative connotation. "Pacifism", however, being derived from pax and facio, designates "peace making" and is therefore a positive rather than a negative doctrine. It might be called creative peaceableness.

Howard H. Brinton "The Nature of Quakerism" Pendle Hill Pamphlet #47 P7&8

From Among the Hills (excerpt)

Along the roadside, like the flowers of gold
That tawny Incas for their gardens wrought,
Heavy with sunshine droops the golden-rod,
And the red pennons of the cardinal-flowers
Hang motionless upon their upright staves.
  The sky is hot and hazy, and the wind,
Wing-weary with its long flight from the south,
Unfelt; yet, closely scanned, yon maple leaf
With faintest motion, as one stirs in dreams,
Confesses it. The locust by the wall
Stabs the noon-silence with his sharp alarm.
A single hay-cart down the dusty road
Creaks slowly, with its driver fast asleep
On the load's top. Against the neighboring hill,
Huddled along the stonewall's shady side,
The sheep show white, as if a snowdrift still
Defied the dog-star. Through the open door
A drowsy smell of flowers--gray heliotrope,
And white sweet clover, and shy mignonette--
Comes faintly in, and silent chorus lends
To the pervading symphony of peace.

John Greenleaf Whittier

Early Dawn
20 November 1992

How long it takes the sky to become light
On a November morn! The pace of change
Is not perceptible within the range
Of five long, waiting minutes-yet no fright
Is clearly in the way. Nothing is strange.
At steady pace the light and dark exchange
And day, slow but peaceful, conquers the night.

And so it is with human peace and war.
Peace is a day that dawns, however slow,
Until the thought of war receives a "No"
With the slow growth of habit and of law.
Analogies should be pursued with care
But still, truth always has some footprints there.

Kenneth Boulding

The wolf shall live with the lamb,

and the leopard shall lie down
with the kid; and the calf and
the lion cub shall feed together,
and a little child shall lead them

Isaiah

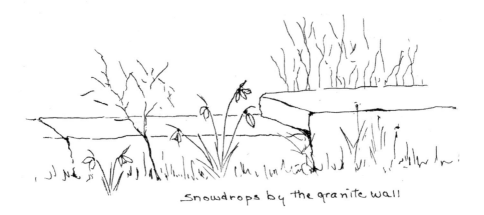

Snowdrops by the granite wall

INTEGRITY

TESTIMONY ON INTEGRITY

Integrity (truth) is a complex concept. Sometimes the word is used for God, sometimes for the conviction that arises from worship, sometimes for the way of life. It was the obedience to truth as they understood it that led Friends to act in ways which others thought odd and even provocative. For early Friends, witnessing to Truth involved the keeping up of public Meetings for Worship, whatever the penalties involved. It also involved preaching, for which many Friends were imprisoned. The concern for truthfulness led Friends right from the first day to refuse to take oaths. An oath according to them was a sign that there were two different levels of truthfulness and they believed that you should tell the truth all the time. Margaret Fell was imprisoned and lost all her property for her refusal to take an oath of loyalty to the king.

Swarthmore Friends Meeting

"IN OUR EVERY DELIBERATION WE MUST
CONSIDER THE IMPACT OF OUR DECISIONS
ON THE NEXT SEVEN GENERATIONS

THE GREAT LAW OF THE SIX NATIONS
IROQUOIS CONFEDERACY

SCRIPTURE ON INTEGRITY

Don't cheat when measuring length, weight, or quantity. Use honest scales and weights and measures. *Leviticus 19:35-36*

Clean living before God and justice with our neighbors
mean far more to God than religious performance. *Proverbs 21:3*

You can't worship two gods at once. Loving one god, you'll end up hating the other. Adoration of one feeds contempt for the other. You can't worship God and Money both. *Matthew 6:24*

You're fortunate if your behavior and your belief are coherent. But if you're not sure, if you notice that you are acting in ways inconsistent with what you believe—some days trying to impose your opinions on others, other days just trying to please them— then you know that you're out of line. If the way you live isn't consistent with what you believe, then it's wrong. *Romans 14:22-23*

But what happens when we live God's way? He brings gifts into our lives, much the same way that fruit appears in an orchard—things like affection for others, exuberance about life, serenity. We develop a willingness to stick with things, a sense of compassion in the heart, and a conviction that a basic holiness permeates things and people. We find ourselves involved in loyal commitments, not needing to force our way in life, able to marshal and direct our energies wisely. *Galatians 5:22-23*

No prolonged infancies among us, please. We'll not tolerate babes in the woods, small children who are an easy mark for impostors. God wants us to grow up, to know the whole truth and tell it in love—like Christ in everything. *Ephesians 4:14-15*

YEARLY MEETING QUERIES ON INTEGRITY

In what way is my life out of harmony with truth as I know it?
Baltimore Yearly Meeting

Do I seek ways to be open to others' opinions without weakening my commitment to critical thinking, intellectual rigor, and truth-seeking? *Earlham College*

Do I seek the truth, and speak it even when it is difficult? *Earlham College*

Does your daily work use means and serve goals which are consistent with the teachings of Jesus? *New England Yearly Meeting*

Do you refuse to let the prevailing culture and media dictate your needs and values? *Northwest Yearly Meeting*

How do I strive to maintain the integrity of my inner and outer lives—in my spiritual journey, my work, and my family responsibilities? *Philadelphia Yearly Meeting*

Are we punctual in keeping promises, just in payment of debts, and honorable in all our dealings? *Southeastern Yearly Meeting*

FRIENDLY VOICES ON INTEGRITY

When people came to have experience of Friends' honesty and truthfulness, and found that their Yea was yea, and their Nay was nay; that they kept to a word in their dealings, and that they would not cozen and cheat them; but that if they sent a child to their shops for anything, they were as well used as if they had come themselves; the lives and conversations of Friends did preach, and reached to the witness of God in the people. *George Fox, 1653*

It is time that Christians were judged more by their likeness to Christ than their notions of Christ. Were this sentiment generally admitted we should not see such tenacious adherence to what men deem the opinions and doctrines of Christ while at the same time in every day practise is exhibited anything but a likeness to Christ. *Lucretia Mott*

The enlightened conscience, disciplined by subjection to the Will of God, is always the final authority and the final guide, upon whose judgments we must rely. Conscience will not betray the highest that we know through these other means. None the less our personal judgment must always be open to the correcting influence of a still deeper insight into God's will-otherwise our "freedom" will degenerate into license." *Howard E. Collier "The Quaker Meeting" Pendle Hill Pamphlet #26 P15*

We do not have to dispute with men about doctrines, and we do not have to argue whether this or that church or this or that religion is right; none of that matters. What matters is that people heard the word and tried to live obedient to the light of truth, hope and love in which the living God showed himself.
Emil Fuchs "Christ in Catastrophe" Pendle Hill Pamphlet #49 P22

A spiritual life, without a very large allowance of disquietude in it, is no spiritual life at all. It is but a flattering superstition of self-love.
Frederick Faber "Self-Deceit: A Comedy On Lies; A Way Of Overcoming Them" Pendle Hill Pamphlet # 50 P10

We are to take truth for our authority, and not authority for truth.
Margaret Hope Bacon "Lucretia Mott Speaking" Pendle Hill Pamphlet #234 P25-26

First Day Thoughts

In calm and cool and silence, once again
I find my old accustomed place among
My brethren, where, perchance, no human tongue
Shall utter words; where never hymn is sung,
Nor deep-toned organ blown, nor censer swung,
Nor dim light falling through the pictured pane!
There, syllabled by silence, let me hear
The still small voice which reached the prophet's ear;
Read in my heart a still diviner law
Than Israel's leader on his tables saw!
There let me strive with each besetting sin,
Recall my wandering fancies, and restrain
The sore disquiet of a restless brain;
And, as the path of duty is made plain,
May grace be given that I may walk therein,
Not like the hireling, for his selfish gain,
With backward glances and reluctant tread,
Making a merit of his coward dread,
But, cheerful, in the light around me thrown,
Walking as one to pleasant service led;
Doing God's will as if it were my own,
Yet trusting not in mine, but in His strength alone!

John Greenleaf Whittier

Sonnet for Science
16 March 1992

Even great scientists have made mistakes,
Which others-often pupils-have corrected;
Science at large expects the unexpected,
Unusual accidents and lucky breaks,
But what it cannot tolerate is fakes.
Lies and deceit, once they have been detected,
Are not forgiven. Totally ejected
From the professions are the found-out rakes.

Another principle that must pervade
The realm of science is that change in views
Must never come from those who threats will use;
Only the power of evidence must persuade.
And freedom to explore and to debate
Must be enjoyed, or science will stagnate.

Kenneth Boulding

EVERY VIOLATION OF TRUTH IS NOT ONLY A SORT OF SUICIDE IN THE LIAR BUT IS A STAB AT THE HEALTH OF HUMAN SOCIETY RALPH WALDO EMERSON

COMMUNITY

TESTIMONY ON COMMUNITY

As equally beloved children of God, all human beings are brothers and sisters, one human family, no matter how great our differences of experience, of culture, of age, of understanding. Friends have found that the Light may illuminate a gathered group as well as an individual heart and bind the group together in a community of faith, conscience and experience. Friends see it as their task to build a broader community throughout our world, by seeing and affirming in each other the divine potential, the Seed, the Christ, the Light within. We must learn to deal with one another by affirming and nurturing the best we find in each other - or, in the words of George Fox - by "answering that of God in everyone". In such a community, Friends believe, human beings witness to the sovereignty, compassion and love of the God of their experience.

Swarthmore Friends Meeting

The only Chain that we can stand
is the Chain from hand to hand
spiritual "Hold On"

SCRIPTURE ON COMMUNITY

You're here to be light, bringing out the God-colors in the world. God is not a secret to be kept. We're going public with this, as public as a city on a hill. If I make you light-bearers, you don't think I'm going to hide you under a bucket, do you? I'm putting you on a light stand. Now that I've put you there on a hilltop, on a light stand—shine! *Matthew 5:14-16*

Jesus said, "'Love the Lord your God with all your passion and prayer and intelligence.' This is the most important, the first on any list. But there is a second to set alongside it: 'Love others as well as you love yourself.' These two commands are pegs; everything in God's Law and the Prophets hangs from them. *Matthew 22:37-40*

In this way, we are like the various parts of a human body. Each part gets its meaning from the body as a whole, not the other way around. The body we're talking about is Christ's body of chosen people. Each of us finds our meaning and function as a part of his body.
Romans 12:4-5

If you've gotten anything at all out of following Christ, if his love has made any difference in your life, if being in a community of the Spirit means anything to you, if you have a heart, if you care— then do me a favor: Agree with each other, love each other, be deep-spirited friends. *Philippians 2:1-2*

Let the peace of Christ keep you in tune with each other, in step with each other. None of this going off and doing your own thing. *Colossians 3:15*

You can develop a healthy, robust community that lives right with God and enjoy its results only if you do the hard work of getting along with each other, treating each other with dignity and honor. *James 3:18*

YEARLY MEETING QUERIES ON COMMUNITY

Are love and harmony within the Meeting community fostered by a spirit of open sharing? *Baltimore Yearly Meeting*

Do I strive to promote a community life that will foster the intellectual, physical, moral, and emotional wellbeing of all members? *Earlham College*

Do you share each other's joys and burdens? *New England Yearly Meeting*

Do we make ourselves available in a tender and caring way when we sense a need for assistance in time of trouble? *New York Yearly Meeting*

Do patience and consideration govern your interactions; and when differences arise, do you resolve them promptly in a spirit of forgiveness and understanding? *Northwest Yearly Meeting*

Do we respect that of God in each person, though it may be expressed in unfamiliar ways or may be difficult for us to discern? *Southeastern Yearly Meeting*

Are we patient and considerate towards those we find difficult to understand or like? *Southeastern Yearly Meeting*

FRIENDLY VOICES ON COMMUNITY

Now the Lord God opened to me by his invisible power that every man was enlightened by the divine light of Christ, and I saw it shine through all; and they that believed in it came out of condemnation to the light of life, and became the children of it; but they that hated it, and did not believe in it, were condemned by it, though they made a profession of Christ. This I saw in the pure openings of the Light without the help of any man; neither did I then know where to find it in the Scriptures; though afterwards, searching the Scriptures, I found it. For I saw in that Light and Spirit which was before Scripture was given forth... that all must come to that Spirit, if they would know God, or Christ, or the Scriptures aright.
George Fox, 1648

If you would know God, and worship and serve God as you should do, you must come to the means He has ordained and given for that purpose. Some seek it in books, some in learned men, but what they look for is in themselves, yet they overlook it. The voice is too still, the Seed too small, and the Light shineth in darkness....The woman that lost her silver found it at home after she had lighted her candle and swept her house. Do you so too, and you shall find what Pilate wanted to know, viz., Truth. The Light of Christ within, who is the Light of the world, and so a light to you that tells you the truth of your condition, leads all that take heed unto it out of darkness into God's marvelous light; for light grows upon the obedient.
William Penn, 1694

And as many candles lighted, and put in one place, do greatly augment the light and make it more to shine forth; so when many are gathered together into the same life, there is more of the glory of God, and his Power appears, to the refreshment of each individual, for that he partakes not only of the light raised in himself, but in all the rest. *Robert Barclay 1678*

It was [Christ's] faith that, if you get into the world anywhere a seed of the Kingdom, a nucleus of persons who exhibit the blessed life, who are dedicated to expanding goodness, who rely implicitly on love and sympathy, who try in meek patience the slow method that is right, who still feel the clasping hands of love even when they go through pain and trial and loss, this seed-spirit will spread, this nucleus will enlarge and create a society. *Rufus Jones 1916*

The Society of Friends took the position that the source of guidance was not merely an individual light but the "sense of the meeting," in other words a communal light. This communal light which illumined a group was reached in a spirit of worship through which each individual aspired to a super-individual level of reality where all individual lights merged into one.
Howard H. Brinton "A Religious Solution to the Social Problem" Pendle Hill Pamphlet #2 P9

One of the immediate and important objects of the Quaker Meeting is to create a Christian "fellowship." If we go to meeting to get what we can out of it, we can be sure of getting very little. If we go to share in its service we shall not come away empty.
Howard E. Collier "The Quaker Meeting" Pendle Hill Pamphlet #26 P9

If we can share other people's joys and happiness, we find an important link uniting us with them. If we cannot, we will be separated from them- even if we do mighty works to help them in their need.
Emil Fuchs "Christ in Catastrophe" Pendle Hill Pamphlet #49 P18

In gospel order, those gathered into the church-community have a covenant with God. It is a living relationship of trust, listening, and responsiveness to God's call. They also have a covenantal relationship comprising the same qualities with each other. They are accountable to God and each other for maintaining these relationships.
Sandra Cronk "Gospel Order: A Quaker Understanding of Faithful Church Community" Pendle Hill Pamphlet #297 P22

Sonnet for the Modern World
11 March 1992

I must confess myself a citizen
Of the blatant world of modernity.
Some of its aspects-its complexity,
Its dominance-make me feel alien,
Longing perhaps, for simpler worlds again,
Disturbed by world-wide uniformity,
Destroying local life in its variety,
Drowning all ancient lands in a vast new sea.

And yet I can't renounce my citizenship,
For I am part of that enormous growth
In knowledge, based on evidence, not oath,
That made the world that has us in its grip.
Ignorance cannot save us-we must find
Knowledge in all the lives of humankind.

Kenneth Boulding

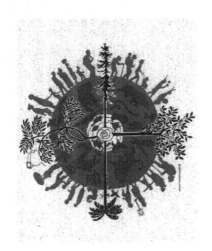

EQUALITY

TESTIMONY ON EQUALITY

If God is directly accessible to all persons, regardless of age, gender, race, nationality, economic, social or educational position - if every person is held equal in God's love and has equal potential to be a channel for the revelation of God's Truth - then all persons are to be equally valued. There is that Seed, that Light - there is "that of God" in every person. For Friends this insight has meant, from the beginning, equality of the sexes and of races. In England and the English colonies, this had to mean the end of privilege based on wealth or class. In Japan and Kenya, where the existing cultures made women little more than 'domestic property', it resulted in the establishment of Quaker schools for girls. It also formed the basis for opposition to slavery and the death penalty.

Swarthmore Friends Meeting

SCRIPTURE ON EQUALITY

God created human beings;
he created them godlike,
Reflecting God's nature.
He created them male and female.
Genesis 1:27

The Life-Light was the real thing:
Every person entering Life
He brings into Light.
John 1:9

Peter fairly exploded with his good news: "It's God's own truth, nothing could be plainer: God plays no favorites! It makes no difference who you are or where you're from—if you want God and are ready to do as he says, the door is open."
Acts 10:34-35

Each person is given something to do that shows who God is: Everyone gets in on it, everyone benefits. All kinds of things are handed out by the Spirit, and to all kinds of people!
1 Corinthians 12:7

In Christ's family there can be no division into Jew and non-Jew, slave and free, male and female. Among us you are all equal. That is, we are all in a common relationship with Jesus Christ. *Galatians 3:28*

YEARLY MEETING QUERIES ON EQUALITY

Do you walk cheerfully over the world, answering that of God in every one?
New England Yearly Meeting

Do you respect the value of all useful work, whether paid or unpaid, whether physical or intellectual, whether performed in the home or in the larger community?
New England Yearly Meeting

Do we acknowledge the oneness of humanity and foster a loving spirit toward all people? *New York Yearly Meeting*

Do we honor Friends' traditional testimony that men and women are equal?
New York Yearly Meeting

Do you recognize the equality of persons regardless of race, gender, or economic status? *Northwest Yearly Meeting*

Do I examine myself for aspects of prejudice that may be buried, including beliefs that seem to justify biases based on race, gender, sexual orientation, disability, class, and feelings of inferiority or superiority? *Philadelphia Yearly Meeting*

Do we acknowledge and support all relationships and families, whether conventional or not, that are based on love and commitment? *Southeastern Yearly Meeting*

FRIENDLY VOICES ON EQUALITY

Men - their rights and nothing more; Women - their rights and nothing less.
Susan B Anthony

My brothers! I am happy to meet you. I have long desired this opportunity to talk with you, but my duty to other tribes has prevented my being with you till this day. I call you brothers because we have all one common father. The Great Creator of all made the white man, the red man and the black man equal. He gave to the white man no more natural rights than He gave to the red man; and I claim from you no rights and privileges but such as I extend to you, and you should claim from me no more than you extend to me. I have long waited to have a plain talk with you, and am glad to see so many here today.
Enoch Hoag, 1869

Love was the first motion, and thence a concern arose to spend some time with the Indians, that I might feel and understand their life and the spirit they live in, if haply I might receive some instruction from them, or they be in any degree helped forward by my following the leadings of truth amongst them. *John Woolman 1763*

And some men say, "Men must have the Power and superiority over the woman, because God says, 'The man must rule over his wife, and that man is not of woman, but the woman is of the man'" (Gen 3:16). Indeed, after man fell, that command was. But before man fell, there was no such command. For they were both meet-helps. They were both to have dominion over all that God made. . . And as man and woman are restored again, by Christ, up into the image of God, they both have dominion again in Righteousness and Holiness, and are helps-meet, as before they fell.
George Fox

Sonnet for Genetics
June 2 1992

In view of all the countless genes we share
All men, quite literally, are my brother,
All women, like my sisters or my mother,
Going right back to the ancestral pair.
The genes that foster love and tender care
And pushed our forebears into being lovers,
We share with them. Then there are many others
That everyone's uniqueness have to bear.
The genes that gave us gender, color, race
Are but a tiny fraction of the whole;
In many ways we share a single soul.
These basic facts our cultures have to face:
If we deny humanity to any,
We do it to ourselves, for each is many.
Kenneth Boulding

keeping faith
that the message of PEACE
filling heart and mind
has power to transform,
bringing goodwill and justice
to all humankind

the children's "Heifer Project" Meal

STEWARDSHIP
(OR SERVICE)

STEWARDSHIP OF THE EARTH TESTIMONY

Friends worldwide have accepted the idea that the testimony of equality in the economic realm implies a commitment to the right sharing of the world's resources. We recognize that the well-being of the Earth is a fundamental spiritual concern. From the beginning, it was through the wonders of nature that people saw God. How we treat the Earth and its creatures is a basic part of our relationship with God. Our planet as a whole, not just the small parts of it in our immediate custody, requires our responsible attention. Friends are indeed called to walk gently on the Earth. Wasteful and extravagant consumption is a major cause of destruction of the environment. Friends are called to become models and patterns of simple living and concern for the Earth.

Swarthmore Friends Meeting

SCRIPTURE ON STEWARDSHIP

God spoke: "Let us make human beings in our image, make them reflecting our nature so they can be responsible for the fish in the sea, the birds in the air, the cattle, and, yes, Earth itself, and every animal that moves on the face of Earth." *Genesis 1:26*

God claims Earth and everything in it, God claims World and all who live on it. *Psalms 24:1*

Never walk away from someone who deserves help; your hand is God's hand for that person. *Proverbs 3:27*

Just then he (Jesus) looked up and saw the rich people dropping offerings in the collection plate. Then he saw a poor widow put in two pennies. He said, "The plain truth is that this widow has given by far the largest offering today. All these others made offerings that they'll never miss; she gave extravagantly what she couldn't afford—she gave her all!" *Luke 21:1-4*

Does merely talking about faith indicate that a person really has it? For instance, you come upon an old friend dressed in rags and half-starved and say, "Good morning, friend! Be clothed in Christ! Be filled with the Holy Spirit!" and walk off without providing so much as a coat or a cup of soup—where does that get you? Isn't it obvious that God-talk without God-acts is outrageous nonsense? *James 2:14-17*

Most of all, love each other as if your life depended on it. Love makes up for practically anything. Be quick to give a meal to the hungry, a bed to the homeless—cheerfully. Be generous with the different things God gave you, passing them around so all get in on it.
I Peter 4:8-10

YEARLY MEETING QUERIES ON STEWARDSHIP
(CARING FOR EACH OTHER)

Do we regard our time, talents, energy, money, material possessions and other resources as gifts from God, to be held in trust and shared according to the Light we are given? *Baltimore Yearly Meeting*

Are you frugal in your personal life and committed to the just distribution of the world's resources? *New England Yearly Meeting*

Do we strive to find, to understand, and to remove causes of misery and suffering? *New York Yearly Meeting*

Do I simplify my needs, making choices that balance self-sufficiency (to avoid unnecessary dependence on others) and fair sharing of resources? *Philadelphia Yearly Meeting*

YEARLY MEETING QUERIES ON STEWARDSHIP
(CARING FOR THE EARTH)

How do we avoid misusing the land, air, and sea and to use the world's resources with care and consideration for future generations and with respect for all life?
Baltimore Yearly Meeting

Do we support measures to establish the conservation and right use of natural resources? *New York Yearly Meeting*

As a Christian steward, do you treat the earth with respect and with a sense of God's splendor in creation, guarding it against abuse by greed, misapplied technology, or your own carelessness? *Northwest Yearly Meeting*

How am I helping to develop a social, economic, and political system which will nurture an environment which sustains and enriches life for all?
Philadelphia Yearly Meeting

FRIENDLY VOICES ON STEWARDSHIP
(CARING FOR EACH OTHER)

If there is any kindness I can show, or any good thing I can do to any fellow being, let me do it now, and not deter or neglect it, as I shall not pass this way again.
William Penn

Of the interest of the public in our estates: Hardly anything is given us for ourselves, but the public may claim a share with us. But of all we call ours, we are most accountable to God and the public for our estates: In this we are but stewards, and to hoard up all to ourselves is great injustice as well as ingratitude. *John Woolman 1720*

Our gracious Creator cares and provides for all his creatures. His tender mercies are over all his works and so far as true love influences our minds, so far we become interested in his workmanship and feel a desire to make use of every opportunity to lessen the distresses of the afflicted and to increase the happiness of the creation. Here we have the prospect of one common interest from which our own is inseparable, that to turn all we possess into the channel of universal love becomes the business of our lives. *John Woolman 1763*

Our task is to bind up the brokenhearted, to be a cup of strength in times of agony, to set men on their feet when the foundations seem to be caving in and to feed and comfort the little children amidst the wreckage of war and devastation.
Rufus Jones "Rethinking Quaker Principles" Pendle Hill Pamphlet # 8 P24 and 25

Sonnet for Maintenance
24 April 1992

Time is a nibbler, and all things decay,
Mountains erode, and rivers fill with silt,
And every temple humankind has built
Crumbles. Our precious bodies turn to clay,
All colors fade and turn into a gray,
And every lovely flower is doomed to wilt,
Edifices of pride crack into guilt,
Garbage accumulates and garments fray.

So let us always give unstinting praise
To those who heal the endless wounds of time,
Braves souls who deal with garbage and with grime,
And fix and mend and heal in many ways.
Always to make new things makes little sense
If we neglect the work of maintenance.
Kenneth Boulding

To be informed ask the animals
Learn from the birds of the air
Speak to the Earth—it has lessons to teach
The fishes of the sea will tell all
Job

FRIENDLY VOICES ON STEWARDSHIP
(CARING FOR THE EARTH)

It would go a long way to caution and direct people in their use of the world, that they were better studied and knowing in the Creation of it. For how could [they] find the confidence to abuse it, while they should see the Great Creator stare them in the face, in all and every part thereof? *William Penn*

The produce of the earth is a gift from our gracious creator to the inhabitants, and to impoverish the earth now to support outward greatness appears to be an injury to the succeeding age. *John Woolman 1772*

Sonnet for the Turning Earth
21 January 1993

How good it is to live on Earth that turns,
That endlessly repeats the simple play
That gives us the great plot of night and day,
Sunrise, noontide, and sunset, and so earns
For us the precious skill that learns
To see the patterns in time's brave display
And so prevents our plans from going astray,
So we don't dash into a fire that burns.

Good it is too that Earth goes round the sun
In annual cycles, giving blessed seasons
So that we search successfully for reasons
Even though in some patterns we may see none.
So it is clear that what makes human worth
At least in part is learned from Mother Earth.

Kenneth Boulding

BRIEF NOTES ON FRIENDLY VOICES

(Numbers after names refer to page number in book where their words are found)

Susan B. Anthony (37)
(February 15, 1820 – March 13, 1906)
Quaker women's rights advocate who worked to give 19th century American women the right to vote

Margaret Bacon (22)
(April 7, 1921-February 24, 2011)
Quaker historian, author and lecturer known especially for books and writings on Quaker women

Robert Barclay (29)
(December 23, 1648-October 3, 1690)
Scottish Quaker who affirmed the Inner Light of Christ as superior to scripture

Kenneth Boulding (7, 13, 15, 23, 31, 38, 45, 46)
(January 18, 1910 – March 18, 1993)
Quaker peace activist, poet, economist and philosopher

Howard Brinton (v, 5-6, 6, 14, 30)
(1884-1973)
Quaker author and teacher who served, along with his wife Anna, as co-director of Pendle Hill religious center in Wallingford Pennsylvania from 1936 to 1949

Howard E. Collier (21, 30)
(1890-1953)
Quaker author and physician, delivered 1936 Swarthmore lecture: "Toward a New Manner of Living"

Sandra Cronk (30)
(1942-2000)
Quaker author, storyteller, spiritual guide and co-founder of the School of the Spirit, a ministry of prayer and learning under the auspices of Philadelphia Yearly Meeting.

Frederick Faber (21)
(1814-1863)
British theologian and hymn writer, best known for hymns "Faith of Our Fathers" and "There's a Wideness in God's Mercy"

Margaret Fell (iv)
(1614 – April 23, 1702)
Along with her husband, George Fox, a founder of the Religious Society of Friends

George Fox (13, 21, 29, 37)
(July 1624 – January 1691)
English founder of the Religious Society of Friends, also known as Quakers or Friends.

Emil Fuchs (21, 30)
(1876-1971)
Lutheran minister and a pacifist who converted to Quakerism in 1925

Richard Gregg (6)
(1885-1974) American philosopher noted for contributions to nonviolent resistance, influenced the thinking of Martin Luther King, Jr and other social reformers

Enoch Hoag (37)
(1812-1884)
Quaker who served as Superintendent under President Grant's Peace Policy to care for Native American tribes in Kansas and Indian territory by building schools, distributing supplies and maintaining peace between tribes and whites

Rufus Jones (6, 30, 44)
(January 25, 1863–June 16, 1948)
Influential Quaker historian, theologian and philosopher

Lucretia Mott (21, 22)
(January 3, 1793 – November 11, 1880)
American Quaker, abolitionist and advocate for women's rights, instrumental in organizing women's rights convention at Seneca Falls, New York in 1848

A. J. Muste (13)
(January 8, 1885 – February 11, 1967)
Quaker activist involved in pacifist, labor and the US civil rights movements

William Penn (5, 29, 44, 46)
(October 14, 1644 – July 30, 1718)
Quaker entrepreneur and philosopher, founder of colony of Pennsylvania, planned and developed city of Philadelphia, noted for his good relations and successful treaties with Delaware Indian tribe

John Greenleaf Whittier (14, 22)
(December 17, 1807 – September 7, 1892)
American Quaker poet and abolitionist

John Woolman (5, 13, 37, 44, 46)
(October 19, 1720 – October 7, 1772)
American Quaker who traveled through the American colonies preaching against slavery and military taxation and conscription

PERMISSIONS AND ACKNOWLEDGMENTS

Scripture
Eugene H. Peterson, The Message: The Bible in Contemporary Language, Copyright
2002, NavPress Publishing Group, Colorado Springs, Colorado, *www.navpress.com*

Queries, Testimonies and Voices

Baltimore Yearly Meeting of the Religious Society of Friends, Faith & Practice, 17100
Quaker Lane, Sandy Spring, Maryland 20860
(Queries used are in a draft status until at least Annual Session held in the summer of
2013) *www.bym-rsf.org*

Earlham College, Community Principles and Practices 2010, 801 National Road West,
Richmond, Indiana 47374-4095 www.earlham.edu/*policies/principles.html*

New England Yearly Meeting of Friends of the Religious Society of Friends, Faith &
Practice 1986, 901 Pleasant Street, Worcester, MA 01602 *www.neym.org*

New York Yearly Meeting of the Religious Society of Friends, Faith & Practice 1998,
15 Rutherford Place, New York, NY 10003 *www.nyym.org*

Northwest Yearly Meeting of the Religious Society of Friends, Faith & Practice 2009,
200 N. Meridian Street, Newberg, OR 97132 *www.nwfriends.org*

Philadelphia Yearly Meeting of the Religious Society of Friends, Faith & Practice
2002, 1515 Cherry Street, Philadelphia, PA 19102 *www.pym.org*

Southeastern Yearly Meeting of the Religious Society of Friends, Faith & Practice
2005, P.O. Box 510795, Melbourne Beach, FL 32951 *www.seym.org*

Swarthmore Monthly Meeting of the Religious Society of Friends, April 2011
testimonies ,12 Whittier Place, Swarthmore PA 19081 *www.swarthmore.quaker.org*

A Religious Solution to the Social Problem Pendle Hill Pamphlet #2. Wallingford, PA: Pendle Hill Publications, 2004

The Value of Voluntary Simplicity: Pendle Hill Pamphlet #3. Wallingford, PA: Pendle Hill Publications, 2004

Rethinking Quaker Principles: Pendle Hill Pamphlet # 8. Wallingford, PA: Pendle Hill Publications, 2002

New Nations for Old: Pendle Hill Pamphlet #17. Wallingford, PA: Pendle Hill Publications, 2002

The Quaker Meeting: Pendle Hill Pamphlet #26. Wallingford, PA: Pendle Hill Publications, 2003

Our Hearts Are Restless: Pendle Hill Pamphlet #32. Wallingford, PA: Pendle Hill Publications, 2002

The Nature of Quakerism: Pendle Hill Pamphlet #47. Wallingford, PA: Pendle Hill Publications, 2006

Christ in Catastrophe: Pendle Hill Pamphlet #49. Wallingford, PA: Pendle Hill Publications, 2003

Self-Deceit-A Comedy on Lies; A Way of Overcoming Them: Pendle Hill Pamphlet # 50. Wallingford, PA: Pendle Hill Publications, 2003

Lucretia Mott Speaking: Pendle Hill Pamphlet #234. Wallingford, PA: Pendle Hill Publications, 1980
Gospel Order- A Quaker Understanding of Faithful Church Community: Pendle Hill Pamphlet #297. Wallingford, PA: Pendle Hill Publications, 1991

(ALL PAMPHLETS ABOVE AND MANY OTHERS AVAILABLE FROM *www.pendlehill.org.*)

Edward E. Boulding, <u>Sonnets from Later Life 1981-1993</u> (Wallingford, PA: Pendle Hill Publications, 1994)

Howard H. Brinton, <u>Friends for 350 Years</u>, updated by Margaret Hope Bacon (Wallingford, PA: Pendle Hill Publications, 2002,)

Testimonials 2002, Sidwell Friends School, 3825 Wisconsin Ave., NW Washington, DC 20016
http://www.sidwell.edu/about-sfs/quaker-values/testimonies/simplicity/index.aspx

Illustrations

Book cover: *2nd Edition* designed by Keith M. Cowley, *www.wildanimalpublishing.com*

Original photograph of *Winchester*, reproduction colonial cupboard, permission to print given by Nicholas A. Berardis, Jr., Crane Hollow Carpentry (Custom and Reproduction Furniture), Middlebury, CT *www.cranehollowcarpentry.com*

Illustration based on *Winchester* photograph by Ian Newbury

Illustration on page iii of Westerly meetinghouse by Jane Bailey, permission to print given by Westerly Monthly Meeting, 57 Elm Street, Westerly RI 02891

Illustrations on pages 2, 8, 10, 16, 18, 24, 26, 32, 34, 38, 40, 45 by Penny Jackim, permission to print given by Penny Jackim, Ahimsa Graphics, Tiverton, RI 02878

Illustrations on pages 1, 9, 17, 25, 33, 39, 53 by Alice Wills, permission to print given by Westerly Monthly Meeting, 57 Elm Street, Westerly RI 02891 and by her son, Dan Wills, and her grandson, Chris Wills